# Contents


Mexican roll .................................................................................................. 3

Alaskan roll .................................................................................................. 4

Dragon roll .................................................................................................. 6

Rainbow roll .................................................................................................. 7

Seared bonito (katsuo-no tataki) roll ................................................................ 8

Shellfish roll .................................................................................................. 9

Dynamite roll .................................................................................................. 10

Cod tempura roll .................................................................................................. 12

Crab salad roll .................................................................................................. 13

Thai shrimp roll .................................................................................................. 14

Buttery scallop roll .................................................................................................. 15

Fried shrimp roll .................................................................................................. 16

Sweet chili shrimp roll .................................................................................................. 18

Negitoro tempura roll .................................................................................................. 19

Fried avocado roll .................................................................................................. 20

Spicy salmon roll .................................................................................................. 22

Egg roll .................................................................................................. 23

Salmon teriyaki roll .................................................................................................. 24

Spicy crab and mango roll .................................................................................................. 25

Spicy fried mozzarella roll .................................................................................................. 26

Asparagus roll .................................................................................................. 28

Zucchini roll .................................................................................................. 29

Sweet potato tempura roll .................................................................................................. 30

Quinoa salad roll .................................................................................................. 31

Rainbow veggie roll .................................................................................................. 32

Chicken katsu roll .................................................................................................. 33

Chicken sausage roll .................................................................................................. 34

Asparagus and bacon roll .................................................................................................. 35

Taco sushi roll .................................................................................................. 36

Korean-inspired beef roll .................................................................................................. 38

Sweet-and-sour pork roll .................................................................................................. 40

Ginger chicken roll .................................................................................................. 41

Sweet-and-sour pork roll .................................................................................................. 42

**Sushi rice**........................................................................................................ 43

**Preparing seafood** ......................................................................................... 45

**Preparing vegetables and other common items** ......................................... 47

**Sashimi, nigiri, and other sushi dishes** ...................................................... 48

Sashimi ............................................................................................................ 49

Assorted sashimi.............................................................................................. 50

Nigiri sushi ...................................................................................................... 51

Japanese egg omelet nigiri.............................................................................. 52

Salmon nigiri with marinated sweet onion ..................................................... 53

Boiled shrimp nigiri ........................................................................................ 54

Scallop nigiri ................................................................................................... 55

Chicken teriyaki nigiri .................................................................................... 56

Beef with scallion nigiri ................................................................................. 57

Spam nigiri ...................................................................................................... 58

**Temari sushi** .................................................................................................. 60

Marinated tuna (zuke-maguro) temari............................................................ 61

Smoked salmon temari with cucumber ........................................................... 62

Egg and salmon roe temari ............................................................................. 63

**Temaki sushi**.................................................................................................. 64

Traditional hand-rolled sushi .......................................................................... 65

Beef with lettuce temaki.................................................................................. 66

Salad temaki..................................................................................................... 67

**Staples and sauces** ......................................................................................... 68

Spicy mayonnaise sauce.................................................................................. 69

Ginger dressing ............................................................................................... 70

Japanese egg omelet ........................................................................................ 71

Tempura batter ................................................................................................. 73

Ponzu sauce...................................................................................................... 74

Sweet eel sauce ................................................................................................ 75

Spicy mango sauce........................................................................................... 76

Pico de gallo .................................................................................................... 77

Tempura dashi sauce ........................................................................................ 78

Sweet-and-sour sauce....................................................................................... 79

Miso sesame sauce........................................................................................... 80

Peanut sauce ........................................................................................................ 81

Pickling liquid .................................................................................................... 82

Almond sauce ...................................................................................................... 83

Pickled sushi ginger (gari) ................................................................................. 84

Tempura batter bits (agedama or tenkasu) ......................................................... 85

**Gunkanmaki sushi** ............................................................................................ **86**

Buttery corn gunkanmaki .................................................................................... 87

Minced tuna and scallion (negitoro) gunkanmaki .............................................. 88

Salmon roe (ikura) gunkanmaki ......................................................................... 89

Lemony crabmeat gunkanmaki ........................................................................... 90

Corn and tuna with mayo gunkanmaki ............................................................... 91


# Mexican roll

**Yield:** 2 big rolls or 12 pieces

**Prep time:** 35 minutes

**Cook time:** 5 minutes

**Ingredients:**

- 4 medium or large tail-on shrimp, peeled and deveined

- 1 tablespoon cornstarch

- Vegetable oil, for frying

- Tempura batter

- 2 whole nori sheets

- 2 cups sushi rice

- 1 tablespoon spicy mayonnaise sauce

- ½ avocado, cut

- 2 pieces leg-style imitation crabmeat, cut lengthwise

- 1 baby cucumber, cut

- ½ cup pico de gallo

**Directions:**

1. Cut a vertical slice on the belly of the shrimp. Place the shrimp belly-side down on a cutting board and press the shrimp lightly against the board to break the tight muscles and straighten. Dredge the shrimp in the cornstarch.

2. In a deep pan, heat 2 inches of vegetable oil over medium heat until it shimmers. Dip the shrimp into the batter, then fry for 2 minutes, occasionally flipping, until golden. Transfer to a wire rack to drain.

3. Put the makisu on a work surface. Place one sheet of nori on it, shiny-side down. Spread 1 cup of rice evenly over the nori. Place a piece of plastic wrap or parchment paper (about the same size as the makisu) on the rice, and flip so the nori side is up.

4. Spread ½ tablespoon of the mayonnaise sauce in a line across the middle of the nori, and lay 2 shrimp pieces (tails sticking out of the nori) on the sauce. Place half of the avocado, 2 pieces of the imitation crab meat, and 2 sticks of cucumber below the shrimp.

5. Pick up the edge of the makisu and nori it into a tight jelly roll. Let it sit seam-side down for 5 minutes at room temperature. Make another roll with the remaining nori, rice, and filling.

6. Cut each sushi roll into 6 pieces and serve topped with pico de gallo.

**Cooking tip:** to check whether the oil is hot enough to fry, drop in some batter. If it floats with bubbles, the oil is ready.

# Alaskan roll

**Yield** : 2 big rolls or 12 pieces

**Prep time:** 30 minutes

**Cook time:** 1 minute

**Ingredients:**

- 4 asparagus stalks, trimmed and rinsed
- 2 whole nori sheets
- 2 cups sushi rice
- 4 tablespoons roasted sesame seeds
- 4 ounces sashimi-grade salmon, cut
- ½ avocado
- 1 teaspoon wasabi
- 2 tablespoons salmon roe
- Soy sauce (gluten-free if necessary)

**Directions:**

1. on a microwave-safe plate, microwave the wet asparagus, covered, for about 40 seconds, until tender.

2. layout the makisu on a work surface and place one piece of nori on it, shiny-side down. Spread 1 cup of sushi rice evenly over the nori. Sprinkle the rice with 2 tablespoons of sesame seeds.

3. place a piece of plastic wrap or parchment paper (about the same size as the makisu) on the rice and flip so the nori side is up.

4. lay 2 asparagus stalks across the middle of the nori. Arrange half of the salmon and half of the avocado below the asparagus.

5. pick up the edge of the makisu and nori closest to you and roll it over the filling into a tight jelly roll. Let it sit, seam-side down, for 5 minutes at room temperature. Make another roll with the remaining nori, rice, sesame seeds, and filling.

6. Cut each sushi roll into 6 pieces, add a small wasabi mound on the corner of a serving plate and ½ teaspoon of salmon roe on each sushi piece, and serve with a small, shallow dish of soy sauce for each person.

# Dragon roll

**Yield:** 2 big rolls or 12 pieces

**Prep time:** 35 minutes

**Cook time:** 10 minutes

**Ingredients:**

- 2 whole nori sheets
- 2 cups sushi rice
- 4 ounces sashimi-grade tuna
- 1 baby cucumber
- 1 avocado,
- Tempura batter bits
- Spicy mayonnaise sauce

**Directions:**

1. Put the makisu on a work surface. Place one sheet of nori on it, shiny-side down. Spread 1 cup of sushi rice evenly over the nori. Place a piece of plastic wrap or parchment paper (about the same size as the makisu) on the rice and flip so the nori side is up.

2. Arrange half of the tuna across the middle of the nori, and place 2 sticks of cucumber below the tuna.

3. Pick up the edge of the makisu and nori into a tight jelly roll. Remove the wrap and makisu, place the roll seam-side down, and arrange half of the avocado diagonally over the roll to mimic the pattern of dragon scales. Cover the roll with the wrap and hold it tightly to make the avocado stick to the roll firmly. Let it sit for 5 minutes at room temperature. Make another roll with the remaining nori, rice, filling, and topping.

4. Cut each sushi roll into 6 pieces and serve with the batter bits sprinkled on top and a drizzle of the mayonnaise sauce.

**Substitution tip:** if you can get tobiko or masago, top each piece with about ¼ teaspoon of it instead of sprinkling with tempura batter bits.

# Rainbow roll

**Yield:** 2 big rolls or 12 pieces

**Prep time:** 35 minutes

**Cook time:** 15 minutes

**Ingredients:**

- 2 whole nori sheets

- 2 cups sushi rice

- 4 ounces sashimi-grade tuna

- 2 pieces leg-style imitation crabmeat

- 1 baby cucumber

- 4 ounces sliced smoked salmon

- ½ avocado

**Directions:**

1. Place the makisu on a work surface. Place one sheet of nori on it, shiny-side down. Spread 1 cup of sushi rice evenly over the nori. Put a piece of plastic wrap or parchment paper (about the same size as the makisu) on the rice and flip so the nori side is up.

2. Lay half of the tuna across the middle of the nori and arrange 2 pieces of imitation crab meat and 2 sticks of cucumber below the  tuna.

3. Pick up the edge of the makisu and nori into a tight jelly roll.

4. Remove the wrap and makisu, and place the roll seam-side down. Place half of the salmon and avocado slices diagonally next to each other over the roll. Cover the roll with the plastic wrap and hold it tightly to make the salmon and avocado stick to the roll firmly. Let it sit for 5 minutes at room temperature. Make another roll with the remaining nori, rice, filling, and topping.

5. Cut each sushi roll into 6 pieces and serve.

**Cooking tip:** smoked salmon and avocado are easy to tear when you cut. To avoid that, cut the roll through the wrapper (if you use plastic wrap) so the topping keeps its shape.

# Seared bonito (katsuo-no tataki) roll

**Yield:** 4 thin rolls or 24 pieces

**Prep time:** 40 minutes

**Cook time:** 5 minutes

**Ingredients:**

- 2 whole nori sheets, halved
- 2 cups sushi rice
- 4 ounces seared bonito, cut into ½-inch-thick and 2½-inch-long sticks
- 8 scallions, trimmed
- ½ cup marinated sweet onion
- 1 tablespoon peeled, grated fresh ginger ponzu sauce

**Directions:**

1. Put the makisu on a work surface. Place one piece of nori on it, shiny-side down. Spread ½ cup of rice evenly over the nori, leaving a ½-inch border on the far side.
2. Place three pieces of the bonito and 2 scallions across the middle of the rice. Add 1 tablespoon of the onion on top.
3. Pick up the edge of the makisu and nori closest to you, attach  the near edge of the rice to the far edge of the rice, and roll-up. Let it sit, seam-side down, for a few minutes. Make three more rolls with the remaining ingredients.
4. Cut each sushi roll into 6 pieces and serve with a small mound of ginger and a dash of ponzu sauce.

# Shellfish roll

**Yield:** 2 big rolls or 12 pieces

**Prep time:** 35 minutes

**Cook time:** 5 minutes

**Ingredients:**

- 4 medium or large shrimp, tail on, deveined
- 2 whole nori sheets
- 2 cups sushi rice
- 4 tablespoons roasted sesame seeds
- Wasabi
- 1 baby cucumber
- 1(4¼-ounce) can crabmeat, drained
- 6 sashimi-grade scallops, halved horizontally
- 2 tablespoons salmon roe
- Soy sauce (gluten-free if necessary)

**Directions:**

1. Fill a deep pan with water and bring it to a boil over high heat.
2. Skewer the shrimp from head to tail to prevent it from curling when cooked. Boil the shrimp over medium heat for 2 to 3 minutes, until it turns pink.
3. Put the makisu on a work surface and place one sheet of nori on it, shiny-side down. Spread 1 cup of rice evenly over the nori. Sprinkle the rice with 2 tablespoons of sesame seeds. Put a piece of plastic wrap or parchment paper (about the same size as the makisu) on the rice and flip so the nori side is up.
4. With your finger, spread a small amount of wasabi in a line across the middle of the nori. Place 2 shrimp pieces (tails sticking out of the nori) on the wasabi, and place 2 sticks of cucumber, 3 tablespoons of the crab, and 6 pieces of the scallop below the
5. Shrimp.
6. Pick up the edge of the makisu and nori closest to you, and roll into a tight jelly roll. Let it sit, seam-side down, for 5 minutes at room temperature. Make another roll with the remaining nori, rice, sesame seeds, and filling.
7. Cut each sushi roll into 6 pieces, top each piece with ½ teaspoon of the salmon roe, and serve with soy sauce.

# Dynamite roll

**Yield:** 2 big rolls or 12 pieces

**Prep time:** 40 minutes

**Cook time:** 5 minutes

**Ingredients:**

- 4 medium or large tail-on shrimp, deveined
- 1 tablespoon cornstarch
- Vegetable oil, for frying
- Tempura batter
- 1 whole nori sheets
- 2 cups sushi rice
- 4 tablespoons roasted sesame seeds
- 2 tablespoons spicy mayonnaise sauce, divided
- Baby cucumber, cut
- ½ cup bean sprouts washed
- ½ cup shredded red cabbage
- Sweet eel sauce
- ½ cup store-bought crispy fried onions

**Directions:**

1. Make small cuts vertically on the shrimp belly, place belly-side down on a cutting board, and press the shrimp lightly to straighten. Dredge the shrimp in the cornstarch.

2. In a deep pan, heat 2 inches of vegetable oil over medium heat until it shimmers. Dip the shrimp into the batter, then fry for 2 minutes, occasionally flipping, until golden. Transfer to a wire rack to drain.

3. Layout the makisu on a work surface and place one sheet of nori on top, shiny side down. Spread 1 cup of rice evenly over the nori, and sprinkle with 2 tablespoons of sesame seeds. Put a piece of plastic wrap or parchment paper (about the same size as the makisu) on the rice and flip so the nori side is up.

4.  Spread about ½ tablespoon of the mayonnaise sauce across the middle of the nori. Place 2 shrimp, tails sticking out of the nori, on the sauce, and arrange 2 sticks of cucumber, ¼ cup of the sprouts, and ¼ cup of the cabbage below the shrimp.

5.  Pick up the edge of the makisu and nori into a tight jelly roll. Let it sit, seam-side down, for 5 minutes at room temperature. Make another roll with the remaining nori, rice, sesame seeds, and filling.

6.  Cut each sushi roll into 6 pieces and top each piece with a dash of mayonnaise sauce, a drizzle of the eel sauce, and a sprinkle of fried onions.

# Cod tempura roll

**Yield:** 4 thin rolls or 24 pieces

**Prep time:** 40 minutes

**Cook time:** 20 minutes

**Ingredients:**

- 1 (½ pound) cod fillet, cut into
- 2½-inch-thick sticks
- 2 tablespoons cornstarch
- Vegetable oil, for frying
- Tempura batter
- 16 green beans, trimmed
- 2 whole nori sheets, halved
- 2 cups sushi rice
- Soy sauce (gluten-free if necessary)

**Directions:**

1. Lay the cod on paper towels and blot dry. Dust the cod lightly with the cornstarch.
2. In a deep pan, heat 2 inches of vegetable oil over medium-low heat until it shimmers. Dip the cod into the batter, then fry for 4 minutes, occasionally flipping, until golden. Transfer to a wire rack to drain.
3. Dip the green beans into the batter, then fry for 2 to 3 minutes, flipping occasionally. Transfer to a wire rack to drain.
4. Put the makisu on a work surface. Place one piece of nori on it, shiny-side down. Spread ½ cup of sushi rice evenly over the nori, leaving a ½-inch border on the far side.
5. Across the middle of the rice, place one-quarter of the cod tempura and 4 green beans.
6. Pick up the edge of the makisu and nori closest to you, attach the near edge of rice to the far edge of the rice, and roll-up. Let it sit, seam-side down, for a few minutes. Make three more rolls with the remaining nori, rice, and filling.
7. Cut each sushi roll into 6 pieces and serve with soy sauce.

# Crab salad roll

**Yield:** 4 thin rolls or 24 pieces

**Prep time:** 45 minutes

**Cook time:** 7 minutes

**Ingredients:**

- 1 (4¼-ounce) can crabmeat, drained
- 3 tablespoons mayonnaise
- Salt
- Freshly ground black pepper
- 2 whole nori sheets, halved
- 2 cups sushi rice
- 4 tablespoons roasted sesame seeds
- 2 romaine lettuce leaves, halved lengthwise wasabi mayonnaise sauce

**Directions:**

1. In a small bowl, stir together the crabmeat and mayonnaise. Season with salt and pepper.

2. Put the makisu on a work surface and place one piece of nori on it, shiny-side down. Spread ½ cup of rice evenly over the  nori. Sprinkle with 1 tablespoon of sesame seeds. Put a piece of plastic wrap or parchment paper (about the same size as the makisu) on the rice and flip so the nori side is up.

3. Place one piece of lettuce on the nori and place 2 tablespoons of the crabmeat mixture across the middle of the lettuce.

4. Pick up the edge of the makisu and nori into a tight jelly roll. Let it sit, seam-side down, for a few minutes. Make three more rolls with the remaining nori, rice, sesame seeds, and filling.

5. Cut each sushi roll into 6 pieces and drizzle with the mayonnaise sauce.

# Thai shrimp roll

**Yield:** 4 thin rolls or 24 pieces

**Prep time:** 50 minutes

**Cook time:** 5 minutes

**Ingredients:**

- 8 medium shrimp, deveined

- 2 whole nori sheets, halved

- 2 cups sushi rice

- ½ cup bean sprouts washed

- 8 cilantro sprigs, washed and trimmed

- ½ cup peanuts, crushed peanut sauce

**Directions:**

1. Fill a deep pan with water and bring it to a boil over high heat.

2. Skewer the shrimp from head to tail to prevent it from curling when cooked. Boil the shrimp over medium heat for 2 to 3 minutes, until it turns pink.

3. Place the makisu on a work surface and place one piece of nori on it, shiny-side down. Spread ½ cup of rice evenly over the nori. Put a piece of plastic wrap or parchment paper (about the same size as the makisu) on the rice and flip so the nori side is up.

4. Place 2 shrimp across the middle of the nori and arrange one quarter of the sprouts and 2 cilantro sprigs below the shrimp.

5. Pick up the edge of the makisu and nori it into a tight jelly roll. Let it sit, seam-side down, for a few minutes. Make three more rolls with the remaining nori, rice, and filling.

6. Cut each sushi roll into 6 pieces and serve sprinkled with peanuts and the peanut sauce drizzled on top.

# Buttery scallop roll

**Yield:** 2 big rolls or 12 pieces

**Prep time:** 40 minutes

**Cook time:** 20 minutes

**Ingredients:**

- 2 tablespoons butter or margarine
- 12 scallops, halved horizontally
- 8 asparagus stalks, trimmed
- 2 tablespoons soy sauce (gluten-free if necessary)
- ½ cup fresh corn kernels
- 2 whole nori sheets, halved
- 2 cups sushi rice
- 4 tablespoons roasted sesame seeds

**Directions:**

1. In a skillet, melt 1 tablespoon of butter over medium heat. Add half the scallops and half the asparagus, and sauté for 5 minutes, flipping halfway through. Add 1 tablespoon of soy sauce and stir for 2 minutes. Transfer to a plate. Repeat with the remaining butter, scallops, asparagus, and soy sauce.

2. Add the corn to the empty skillet, and stir-fry over medium heat for about 5 minutes while scraping up the seasonings on the bottom of the skillet. Set aside.

3. Layout the makisu on a work surface and place one piece of nori on it, shiny-side down. Spread ½ cup of rice evenly over the nori. Sprinkle with 1 tablespoon of the sesame seeds. Put a piece of plastic wrap or parchment paper (about the same size as the makisu) on the rice and flip so the nori side is up.

4. Lay 2 asparagus stalks across the middle of the nori, and arrange 6 scallop pieces on the asparagus.

5. Pick up the edge of the makisu and nori into a tight jelly roll. Let it sit, seam-side down, for a few minutes. Make three more rolls with the remaining nori, rice, sesame seeds, and filling.

6. Cut each sushi roll into 6 pieces, top each piece with 1 teaspoon of the corn, and serve.

# Fried shrimp roll

**Yield:** 2 big rolls or 12 pieces

**Prep time:** 45 minutes

**Cook time:** 10 minutes

**Ingredients:**

- 1 teaspoon cornstarch
- 1 teaspoon water
- 2 eggs, beaten
- Nonstick cooking spray
- 4 large tail-on shrimp, deveined
- Tablespoons all-purpose flour
- ½ cup bread crumbs
- Vegetable oil, for frying
- Whole nori sheets
- 2 cups sushi rice
- Romaine lettuce leaf halved lengthwise
- Tempura batter bits
- Soy sauce, mayonnaise sauce

**Directions:**

1. In a small dish, whisk together the cornstarch and water. Mix in the beaten egg.

2. Heat an 8-inch nonstick skillet over medium-high heat and coat with cooking spray. Pour half of the egg mixture into the skillet and spread to make a thin layer. Cook over low heat for 3 minutes, flipping halfway through the cooking time. Make a second thin fried egg with the remaining egg mixture.

3. Make small cuts vertically on the shrimp belly, place belly-side down on a cutting board, and press the shrimp lightly to straighten. Bread the shrimp by coating them in the flour, then the egg, and then the bread crumbs.

4. In a deep pan, heat 2 inches of vegetable oil over medium heat until it shimmers. Fry the shrimp for 2 minutes, occasionally flipping, until golden. Transfer to a wire rack to drain.

5. Layout the makisu on a work surface and place one sheet of nori on top, shiny side down. Spread 1 cup of rice evenly over the nori. Put a piece of plastic wrap or parchment paper (about the same size as the makisu) on the rice and flip so the nori side is up.

6. Place a thin fried egg on the nori. Across the middle of the egg, place a piece of lettuce. On top of the lettuce, place 2 shrimp, tails sticking out from the nori.

7. Pick up the edge of the makisu and nori into a tight jelly roll. Let it sit, seam-side down, for 5 minutes at room temperature. Make another roll with the remaining nori, rice, and filling.

8. Cut each sushi roll into 6 pieces, sprinkle with the tempura batter bits, drizzle with the mayonnaise sauce, and serve.

**Cooking tip:** the cornstarch keeps the thin fried egg from tearing. However, if the egg cooks too long, it can shatter.

# Sweet chili shrimp roll

**Yield:** 4 thin rolls or 24 pieces

**Prep time:** 50 minutes

**Cook time:** 5 minutes

**Ingredients:**

- 8 medium shrimp, deveined

- 2 whole nori sheets, halved

- 2 cups sushi rice

- 4 tablespoons roasted sesame seeds

- 2 tablespoons sweet chili sauce

- ½ cup shredded red cabbage

- ½ cup bean sprouts washed

- Sweet chili mayonnaise sauce

**Directions:**

1. Fill a deep pan with water and bring it to a boil over high heat.

2. Skewer the shrimp from head to tail to prevent it from curling when cooked—boil the shrimp over medium heat for 2 to 3 minutes, or until it, turns pink.

3. Put the makisu on a work surface and place one piece of nori on it, shiny-side down. Spread ½ cup of rice evenly over the nori and sprinkle 1 tablespoon of the sesame seeds on top. Put a  piece of plastic wrap or parchment paper (about the same size as the makisu) on the rice and flip so the nori side is up.

4. Spread ½ tablespoon of chili sauce in a line across the middle of the nori. Place 2 shrimp on the sauce. Add one-quarter of the cabbage and one-quarter of the sprouts below the shrimp.

5. Pick up the edge of the makisu and nori into a tight jelly roll. Let it sit, seam-side down, for a few minutes. Make three more rolls with the remaining nori, rice, sesame seeds, and filling.

6. Cut each sushi roll into 6 pieces and drizzle with chili mayonnaise.

# Negitoro tempura roll

**Yield:** 4 thin rolls or 24 pieces

**Prep time:** 50 minutes

**Cook time:** 10 minutes

**Ingredients:**

- 4 ounces sashimi-grade tuna, finely minced
- 1 tablespoon soy sauce (gluten-free if necessary)
- 1 scallion, both white and green parts, chopped
- 2 whole nori sheets, halved
- 2 cups sushi rice
- Vegetable oil, for frying
- Tempura batter
- Tempura dashi sauce

**Directions:**

1. In a mixing bowl, stir together the tuna, soy sauce, and scallion.
2. Layout the makisu on a work surface and place one piece of nori on it, shiny-side down. Spread ½ cup of rice evenly over the nori, leaving a ½-inch border on the far side.
3. Spread 2 tablespoons of the tuna mixture in a line across the middle of the rice.
4. Pick up the edge of the makisu and nori closest to you, attach the near edge of rice to the far side of the rice, and roll-up. Let it sit, seam-side down, until the nori sticks firmly, for a few minutes. Make three more rolls with the remaining nori, rice, and filling.
5. In a deep pan, heat 2 inches of vegetable oil over medium heat until it shimmers. Dip the rolls in the batter, then fry until golden, about 2 to 3 minutes. Transfer to a wire rack to drain. Repeat with the remaining rolls.
6. Cut the sushi roll into 6 pieces and serve with a dish of dashi sauce.

# Fried avocado roll

**Yield:** 2 big rolls or 12 pieces

**Prep time:** 35 minutes

**Cook time:** 10 minutes

**Ingredients:**

- 1 avocado, cut lengthwise into 8 equal pieces
- 3 tablespoons all-purpose flour
- 1 egg, beaten
- ¾ cup bread crumbs
- Vegetable oil, for frying
- 2 whole nori sheets
- 2 cups sushi rice
- 4 tablespoons roasted sesame seeds
- 4 ounces sashimi-grade tuna, cut
- 4 ounces sliced smoked salmon
- Sweet eel sauce

**Directions:**

1. Coat the avocado pieces in the flour, then the beaten egg, and then the bread crumbs.
2. In a deep pan, heat 2 inches of vegetable oil over medium heat until it shimmers. Add the avocado pieces and fry for 2 to 3 minutes, occasionally flipping, until golden. Transfer to a wire rack to drain.
3. Layout the makisu on a work surface and place one sheet of nori on it, shiny-side down. Spread 1 cup of rice evenly over the nori. Sprinkle the rice with 2 tablespoons of sesame seeds. Put a piece
4. Of plastic wrap or parchment paper (about the same size as the makisu) on the rice and flip so the nori side is up.
5. Lay 4 pieces of the avocado across the middle of the nori, and arrange half of the tuna below the avocado.
6. Pick up the edge of the makisu and nori into a tight jelly roll. Remove the wrap and makisu, place the roll seam-side down, and arrange half of the smoked salmon slices next to each other lengthwise over the roll. Cover the roll with the plastic wrap and hold it tightly to make the salmon stick to the

roll firmly. Let it sit for 5 minutes at room temperature. Make another roll with the remaining nori, rice, sesame seeds, filling, and topping.

7. Cut each sushi roll into 6 pieces, drizzle with the sauce, and serve.

**Cleanup tip:** do not drain the used oil down the sink. Instead, stuff paper towels into an empty can or jar for absorption, and pour the cooled oil into the container. Throw the can or jar into the regular garbage.

# Spicy salmon roll

**Yield:** 4 thin rolls or 24 pieces

**Prep time:** 45 minutes

**Cook time:** 12 minutes

**Ingredients:**

- 2 whole nori sheets, halved

- 2 cups sushi rice

- 2 tablespoons spicy mayonnaise sauce

- 1 cup baby arugula

- 4 ounces sashimi-grade salmon, cut

- 3 baby cucumbers, very thinly sliced lengthwise

- Zest of 1 lemon

**Directions:**

1. Layout the makisu on a work surface and place one piece of nori on it, shiny-side down. Spread ½ cup of rice evenly over the nori. Put a piece of plastic wrap or parchment paper (about the same size as the makisu) on the rice and flip so the nori side is up.

2. Spread ½ tablespoon of the sauce in a line across the middle of  the nori. Spread one-quarter of the arugula on top of the sauce, and lay 3 pieces of the salmon on the arugula.

3. Pick up the edge of the makisu and nori into a tight jelly roll. Remove the wrap and makisu, place the roll seam-side down, and arrange the cucumber slices lengthwise on a slight diagonal over the roll. Cover the roll with the plastic wrap and hold it tightly to make the cucumber stick to the roll firmly. Let it sit for a few minutes. Make three more rolls with the remaining nori, rice, and filling.

4. Cut each sushi roll into 6 pieces, sprinkle with lemon zest, and serve.

# Egg roll

**Yield:** 3 thin rolls or 12 pieces

**Prep time:** 35 minutes

**Cook time:** 10 minutes

**Ingredients:**

- 1 teaspoon cornstarch
- 1 teaspoon water
- 1 teaspoon soy sauce (gluten-free if necessary)
- 2 eggs, beaten
- Nonstick cooking spray
- 1 cup sushi rice
- 1½ baby cucumbers, cut
- ½ avocado cut lengthwise into 6 equal pieces

**Directions:**

1. In a small dish, whisk together the cornstarch and water. Mix in the soy sauce and the beaten eggs.

2. Heat an 8-inch nonstick skillet over medium-high heat and coat with cooking spray. Pour one-third of the egg mixture into the skillet and spread the egg over the surface of the skillet to make a thin layer. Cook over low heat for 3 minutes, flipping halfway through. Make two more thin fried eggs with the remaining egg mixture.

3. Layout the makisu on a work surface and place one egg on top. Spread ⅓ cup of rice evenly over half the egg. Press the rice lightly.

4. Place 2 pieces of cucumber and 2 pieces of avocado on the rice.

5. Pick up the edge of the makisu and nori into a tight jelly roll. Let it sit, seam-side down, for a few minutes. Make two more rolls with the remaining eggs, rice, and filling.

6. Cut each sushi roll into 4 pieces and serve.

**Cooking tip:** wrap the makisu with pieces of paper towel, parchment paper, or plastic wrap before placing the fried egg on top. This keeps the makisu from getting oil stains.

# Salmon teriyaki roll

**Yield:** 4 thin rolls or 24 pieces

**Prep time:** 40 minutes

**Cook time:** 10 minutes

**Ingredients:**

- 4 ounces sashimi-grade salmon, cut
- ¼ cup sweet eel sauce
- 2 whole nori sheets, halved
- 2 cups sushi rice
- 4 tablespoons roasted sesame seeds
- 8 parsley sprigs, trimmed
- Wasabi mayonnaise sauce
- 4 scallions, both white and green parts, chopped

**Directions:**

1. In a dry nonstick skillet, cook the salmon over medium-low heat for 4 minutes, flipping occasionally. Add the eel sauce and cook for 2 minutes more, frequently flipping to coat the salmon.

2. Layout the makisu and place one piece of nori on top, shiny side down. Spread ½ cup of rice evenly over the nori. Spread 1 tablespoon of sesame seeds on the rice. Put a piece of plastic wrap or parchment paper (about the same size as the makisu) on the rice and flip so the nori side is up.

3. Arrange 3 pieces of salmon and 2 parsley sprigs across the middle of the nori.

4. Pick up the edge of the makisu and nori into a tight jelly roll. Let it sit, seam-side down, for a few minutes. Make three more rolls with the remaining nori, rice, sesame seeds, and filling.

5. Cut each sushi roll into 6 pieces, drizzle with the sauce, sprinkle with the scallions, and serve.

# Spicy crab and mango roll

**Yield:** 4 thin rolls or 24 pieces

**Prep time:** 45 minutes

**Cook time:** 10 minutes

**Ingredients:**

- 4 ounces cooked crabmeat, coarsely chopped
- 1 teaspoon sweet chili sauce salt
- Freshly ground black pepper
- Juice of ½ lemon
- 2 whole nori sheets, halved
- 2 cups sushi rice
- ½ avocado, cut
- 1 cup spicy mango sauce

**Directions:**

1. In a bowl, stir together the crabmeat, the sweet chili sauce, a pinch of salt and pepper, and the lemon juice.

2. Layout the makisu on a work surface and place one piece of nori on it, shiny-side down. Spread ½ cup of rice evenly over the nori. Put a piece of plastic wrap or parchment paper (about the same size as the makisu) on the rice and flip so the nori side is up.

3. Spread 2 tablespoons of the crab mixture in a line across the middle of the nori. Place 2 or 3 slices of avocado on top of the crab mixture.

4. Pick up the edge of the makisu and nori into a tight jelly roll. Make three more rolls with the remaining nori, rice, and filling.

5. Cut each sushi roll into 6 pieces, top with the mango sauce, and serve.

# Spicy fried mozzarella roll

**Yield:** 2 big rolls or 12 pieces

**Prep time:** 35 minutes

**Cook time:** 2 minutes

**Ingredients:**

- 3 mozzarella cheese sticks, halved
- 2 tablespoons all-purpose flour
- 1 egg, beaten
- ½ cup bread crumbs
- Vegetable oil, for frying
- 2 whole nori sheets
- 2 cups sushi rice
- 4 tablespoons roasted sesame seeds
- 1 romaine lettuce leaf, halved lengthwise
- ½ cup pico de gallo
- Spicy mayonnaise sauce

**Directions:**

1. coat the mozzarella sticks in flour, then egg, and then bread crumbs.

2. in a deep pan, heat 2 inches of vegetable oil over medium heat until it shimmers. Fry the mozzarella, flipping occasionally, until golden, about 30 to 60 seconds. Transfer to a wire rack to drain.

3. layout the makisu on a work surface and place one piece of nori on top, shiny side down. Spread 1 cup of sushi rice evenly over the nori. Spread 2 tablespoons of the sesame seeds on the rice. Put a piece of plastic wrap or parchment paper (about the same size as the makisu) on the rice and flip so the nori side is up.

4. place a piece of lettuce across the middle of the nori. Place 3 pieces of the fried mozzarella on the lettuce, and spread ¼ cup of the pico de gallo in a line below the mozzarella.

5. pick up the edge of the makisu and nori into a tight jelly roll. Let it sit for 5 minutes at room temperature. Make another roll with the remaining nori, rice, sesame seeds, and filling.

6. cut each sushi roll into 6 pieces, drizzle with mayonnaise sauce, and serve.

# Asparagus roll

**Yield:** 4 thin rolls or 24 pieces

**Prep time:** 45 minutes

**Cook time:** 5 minutes

**Ingredients:**

- Vegetable oil, for frying
- 8 asparagus stalks, trimmed and washed
- Tempura batter
- 2 whole nori sheets, halved
- 2 cups sushi rice
- 4 tablespoons roasted sesame seeds
- Japanese egg omelet quartered lengthwise and each quarter halved crosswise
- Miso sesame sauce

**Directions:**

1. In a deep pan, heat 2 inches of vegetable oil over medium-low heat until it shimmers. Dip the asparagus into the batter, then fry for 2 minutes, occasionally flipping, until golden. Transfer to a wire rack to drain.

2. Layout the makisu on a work surface and place one piece of nori on top, shiny side down. Spread ½ cup of rice evenly over the nori. Sprinkle 1 tablespoon of the sesame seeds over the rice. Place a piece of plastic wrap or parchment paper (about the same size as the makisu) on the rice and flip so the nori side is up.

3. Place 2 pieces of asparagus across the middle of the nori and arrange 1 or 2 omelet sticks below the asparagus.

4. Pick up the edge of the makisu and nori into a tight jelly roll. Let it sit, seam-side down, for 2 minutes. Make three more rolls with the remaining nori, rice, sesame seeds, and filling.

5. Cut each sushi roll into 6 pieces, drizzle the sauce on top, and serve.

# Zucchini roll

**Yield:** 4 thin rolls or 24 pieces

**Prep time:** 50 minutes

**Cook time:** 15 minutes

**Ingredients:**

- 1 zucchini, cut into
- ½-inch-thick sticks
- 3 tablespoons all-purpose flour
- 1 egg, beaten
- ¾ cup bread crumbs
- Vegetable oil, for frying
- 2 whole nori sheets, halved
- 2 cups sushi rice
- ¾ (8-ounce) package cream cheese, cut into ½-inch-thick sticks
- 1 avocado, cut
- Freshly ground black pepper

**Directions:**

1. bread the zucchini by rolling it in the flour, then the egg, and then the bread crumbs.

2. in a deep pan, heat 2 inches of vegetable oil over medium heat until it shimmers. Fry the zucchini for 2 to 3 minutes, in batches, if necessary, until golden. Transfer to a wire rack to drain.

3. layout the makisu on a work surface and place one piece of nori on top, shiny side down. Spread ½ cup of rice evenly over the nori. Put a piece of plastic wrap or parchment paper (about the same size as the makisu) on the rice and flip so the nori side is up.

4. arrange 2 or 3 pieces of the zucchini across the middle of the nori. Add 1 or 2 pieces of the cream cheese below the zucchini.

5. pick up the edge of the makisu and nori into a tight jelly roll. Remove the wrap and makisu, place the roll seam-side down, and arrange one-quarter of the avocado slices next to one another lengthwise over the roll. Cover the roll with the plastic wrap and hold it tightly to make the avocado stick to the roll firmly. Let it sit for 5 minutes at room temperature. Make three more rolls with the remaining nori, rice, filling, and topping.

6. Cut each sushi roll into 6 pieces, sprinkle with the black pepper, and serve.

# Sweet potato tempura roll

**Yield:** 2 big rolls or 12 pieces

**Prep time:** 30 minutes

**Cook time:** 15 minutes

**Ingredients:**

- Vegetable oil, for frying
- ½ medium sweet potato, peeled and cut into ½-inch-thick sticks
- Tempura batter
- 4 shiitake mushrooms, stemmed and halved
- 2 whole nori sheets
- 2 cups sushi rice
- 4 tablespoons roasted sesame seeds
- Tempura dashi sauce

**Directions:**

1. In a deep pan, heat 2 inches of vegetable oil over medium-low heat until it shimmers. Dip the sweet potato sticks into the batter, then fry about 4 pieces at a time for 3 minutes, occasionally flipping, until golden. Transfer to a wire rack to drain.

2. Dip the mushrooms into the batter, then fry for 1 to 2 minutes, flipping occasionally. Transfer to a wire rack to drain.

3. Layout the makisu on a work surface and place one sheet of nori on top, shiny side down. Spread 1 cup of sushi rice evenly over the nori. Sprinkle the rice with 2 tablespoons of the sesame seeds. Put a piece of plastic wrap or parchment paper (about the same size as the makisu) on the rice and flip so the nori side is up.

4. Arrange half of the sweet potato tempura in a line across the middle of the nori, and place 4 pieces of the shiitake mushrooms below the sweet potatoes.

5. Pick up the edge of the makisu and nori into a tight jelly roll. Let it sit, seam-side down, for 5 minutes at room temperature. Make another roll with the remaining nori, rice, sesame seeds, and filling.

6. Cut each sushi roll into 6 pieces and serve with a dish of dashi sauce.

# Quinoa salad roll

**Yield:** 2 big rolls or 12 pieces

**Prep time:** 25 minutes

**Cook time:** 10 minutes

**Ingredients:**

- 2 whole nori sheets
- 1 cup cooked quinoa
- ½ cup arugula
- ½ yellow bell pepper, sliced
- 1 medium tomato, seeded and sliced
- ½ avocado
- Almond sauce

**Directions:**

1. Layout the makisu on a work surface and place one sheet of nori on it, shiny-side down. Spread ½ cup of the quinoa evenly over the nori, leaving a 2-inch border on the far side.

2. Place ¼ cup of arugula in a line across the middle of the quinoa. Place half of the bell pepper, half of the tomato, and half of the avocado on the arugula.

3. Pick up the edge of the makisu and nori into a jelly roll. Let it sit for 5 minutes at room temperature. Make another roll with the remaining nori, quinoa, and filling.

4. Cut each sushi roll into 6 pieces, drizzle with almond sauce, and serve.

# Rainbow veggie roll

**Yield:** 2 big rolls or 12 pieces

**Prep time:** 30 minutes, plus 20 minutes to marinate

**Cook time:** 5 minutes

**Ingredients:**

- 1 tablespoon toasted sesame oil
- ½ yellow bell pepper, sliced
- ½ cup pickling liquid
- 2 whole nori sheets
- 2 cups sushi rice
- 4 tablespoons roasted sesame seeds
- 1 romaine lettuce leaf, halved lengthwise
- 1 baby cucumber, cut
- ½ cup shredded red cabbage
- 1 avocado, cut
- Finely ground himalayan pink salt

**Directions:**

1. In a skillet, heat the sesame oil over medium heat until it shimmers. Add the bell pepper and cook for 5 minutes. In a bowl, stir together the bell pepper and the pickling liquid. Let it sit for 20 minutes at room temperature.

2. Lay out the makisu on a work surface and place one sheet of nori on top, shiny side down. Spread 1 cup of sushi rice evenly over the nori. Sprinkle 2 tablespoons of the sesame seeds on top of the rice. Put a piece of plastic wrap or parchment paper (about the same size as the makisu) on the rice and flip so the nori side is up.

3. Lay a piece of the lettuce across the middle of the nori. Place 2 pieces of the cucumber, ¼ cup of the cabbage, and half of the pickled bell pepper on the lettuce.

4. Pick up the edge of the makisu and nori into a tight jelly roll. Remove the wrap and makisu, place the roll seam-side down, and arrange half of the avocado slices side by side lengthwise over the roll. Cover the roll with the wrap, and hold tightly to make the avocado stick to the roll firmly. Let it sit for 5 minutes at room temperature. Make another roll with the remaining nori, rice, sesame seeds, filling, and topping.

5. Cut each sushi roll into 6 pieces, sprinkle with salt, and serve.

# Chicken katsu roll

**Yield:** 4 thin rolls or 24 pieces

**Prep time:** 45 minutes

**Cook time:** 10 minutes

**Ingredients:**

- 6 ounces chicken breast, cut into ½-inch-wide strips
- Salt
- Freshly ground black pepper
- 2 tablespoons all-purpose flour
- 1 egg, beaten
- ½ cup bread crumbs
- Vegetable oil, for frying
- 2 whole nori sheets, halved
- 2 cups sushi rice
- 4 tablespoons roasted sesame seeds
- 1 cup shredded cabbage
- Sweet eel sauce

**Directions:**

1. Season the chicken with salt and pepper.
2. Coat the chicken in the flour, then the egg, and then the bread crumbs.
3. In a deep pan, heat 2 inches of vegetable oil over medium heat until it shimmers. Fry the chicken for about 4 minutes, until golden, flipping occasionally. Transfer to a wire rack to drain.
4. Lay out the makisu on a work surface and place one piece of nori on top, shiny side down. Spread ½ cup of rice evenly over the nori. Sprinkle with 1 tablespoon of sesame seeds. Place a piece of plastic wrap or parchment paper (about the same size as the makisu) on the rice and flip so the nori side is up.
5. Place one-quarter of the chicken across the middle of the nori, and place ¼ cup of the cabbage below the chicken.
6. Pick up the edge of the makisu and nori into a tight jelly roll. Let it sit, seam-side down, for a few minutes. Make three more rolls with the remaining nori, rice, sesame seeds, and filling.
7. Cut each sushi roll into 6 pieces, drizzle with the sauce, and serve.

**Substitution tip:** you can substitute lettuce for cabbage if you prefer.

# Chicken sausage roll

**Yield:** 3 thin rolls or 12 pieces

**Prep time:** 30 minutes

**Cook time:** 15 minutes

**Ingredients:**

- 3 chicken sausages
- 1 teaspoon cornstarch
- 1 teaspoon water1 teaspoon sugar
- 2 eggs, beaten
- Nonstick cooking spray
- 1 cup sushi rice ketchup

**Directions:**

1. Cook the chicken sausages according to the package directions and set aside to cool.

2. In a small dish, whisk together the cornstarch and water. Mix in the sugar and the beaten eggs. Heat an 8-inch nonstick skillet over medium-high heat and coat with cooking spray. Pour one-third of the egg mixture into the skillet and spread the egg all over the surface of the skillet to make a thin layer. Cook over low heat for 3 minutes, gently flipping halfway through the cooking time with a rubber spatula. Make two more thin fried eggs with the remaining egg mixture.

3. Lay out the makisu on a work surface and place one piece of egg on top. Spread ⅓ cup of the rice evenly across half of the egg, and press the rice lightly.

4. Lay 1 sausage across the middle of the rice. Pick up the edge of the makisu and nori into a tight jelly roll. Let it sit, seam-side down, for 2 minutes. Make two more rolls with the remaining egg, rice, and sausage.

5. Cut each sushi roll into 4 pieces, top with a dash of ketchup, and serve.

**Cooking tip:** wrap the makisu with pieces of paper towel, parchment paper, or plastic before placing the fried egg on top to keep the makisu from getting stained.

# Asparagus and bacon roll

**Yield:** 4 thin rolls or 24 pieces

**Prep time:** 40 minutes

**Cook time:** 20 minutes

**Ingredients:**

* 8 turkey bacon slices

* 8 asparagus stalks, trimmed

* 1 tablespoon butter or margarine

* 2 eggs, beaten

* 2 whole nori sheets, halved

* 2 cups sushi rice

* 4 tablespoons roasted sesame seeds

**Directions:**

1. In a dry nonstick skillet, cook the bacon. Transfer to a plate lined with paper towels to drain.

2. In the same skillet, cook the asparagus for 5 minutes, occasionally flipping, until softened slightly. Transfer to a plate.

3. In the skillet, melt the butter. Pour in the beaten egg and cook over medium heat for about 1 minute, moving a spatula across the bottom and sides of the skillet to make small curds. Remove from the heat and set aside.

4. Lay out the makisu on a work surface and place one piece of nori on it, shiny-side down. Spread ½ cup of rice evenly over the nori. Sprinkle the rice with 1 tablespoon of the sesame seeds. Put a piece of plastic wrap or parchment paper (about the same size as the makisu) on the rice and flip so the nori side is up.

5. Lay one piece of bacon across the middle of the nori. On top of the bacon, layer 2 asparagus stalks and another piece of bacon.

6. Pick up the edge of makisu and nori closest to you, and roll into a tight jelly roll. Let it sit, seam-side down, for 2 minutes. Make three more rolls with the remaining nori, rice, sesame seeds, and filling.

7. Cut each sushi roll into 6 pieces, top with the cooked egg, and serve.

# Taco sushi roll

**Yield:** 2 big rolls or 4 pieces

**Prep time:** 25 minutes

**Cook time:** 10 minutes

**Ingredients:**

- 1 tablespoon vegetable oil
- 4 ounces ground beef
- ½ teaspoon onion powder
- ½ teaspoon ground cumin
- ½ teaspoon chili powder
- ½ teaspoon garlic powder
- ½ tablespoon ketchup
- Salt
- Freshly ground black pepper
- 2 whole nori sheets
- 2 cups sushi rice
- ½ cup shredded lettuce
- ½ cup pico de gallo
- ½ cup shredded cheddar cheese

**Directions:**

1. In a skillet, heat the vegetable oil over medium heat until it shimmers. Add the beef and cook, breaking it up with a spatula, until it is browned and no longer pink, about 5 minutes. Drain the excess fat, if any. Season with onion powder, ground cumin, chili powder, garlic powder, ketchup, salt, and pepper. Cook, stirring, for 2 minutes.

2. Put the makisu on a work surface. Place one sheet of nori on it, shiny side down, with the longer side closest to you. Using a wet rice paddle, spread 1 cup of sushi rice evenly over the nori. Leave a 1-inch border on the far side of the nori.

3. Arrange ¼ cup of the beef in a line across the middle of the rice, and lay ¼ cup of the lettuce, ¼ cup of pico de gallo, and ¼ cup of the cheese below the beef.

4.  Pick up the edge of the makisu and nori closest to you, and keep the filling in place with your fingers. Attach the near edge of the rice to the far edge of the rice and roll-up. Hold the roll tightly to form a good shape. Let it sit, seam-side down, for about 5 minutes at room temperature. Make another roll with the remaining nori, rice, and filling.

5.  Wrap the roll with a piece of parchment paper. To serve, halve crosswise at an angle.

6.  **Substitution tip:** you can add avocado or guacamole to the roll as a filling. In that case, reduce the other filling ingredients by half, so the roll will close well.

# Korean-inspired beef roll

**Yield:** 2 big rolls or 12 pieces

**Prep time:** 25 minutes

**Cook time:** 10 minutes

**Ingredients:**

- 4 ounces sirloin steak, chuck steak, or rib-eye steak, cut into ½-inch-thick strips
- Pinch salt, plus 1 teaspoon
- Freshly ground black pepper
- 1 tablespoon vegetable oil
- 2 garlic cloves, minced or grated, divided
- 1 cup bean sprouts, washed
- 1 tablespoon roasted sesame seeds
- 1 tablespoon toasted sesame oil
- 1 teaspoon soy sauce (gluten-free if necessary)
- 1 teaspoon sugar
- 2 whole nori sheets
- 2 cups sushi rice
- 2 scallions, both white and green parts, chopped wasabi mayonnaise sauce

**Directions:**

1. Season the steak with a pinch of salt and black pepper. In a skillet, heat the oil and half of the garlic over medium heat until the garlic starts browning. Cook the beef for 7 to 8 minutes, occasionally flipping, until it browns completely.

2. Microwave the sprouts for 60 to 90 seconds, until tender. Once they're cool enough to handle, squeeze excess water out by hand. In a bowl, stir together the sprouts, the other half of the garlic, sesame seeds, sesame oil, soy sauce, sugar, and 1 teaspoon of salt. Lay out the makisu on a work surface and place one sheet of nori on top, shiny side down. Spread 1 cup of rice evenly over the nori, leaving a 1-inch border on the far side of the nori.

3. Lay half of the steak across the middle of the rice. Arrange half of the sprouts below the beef.

4. Pick up the edge of the makisu and nori, attach the near edge of the rice to the rice on the far side, and roll-up. Let it sit, seam-side down, for about 5 minutes at room temperature. Make another roll with the remaining nori, rice, and filling.

5. Cut each sushi roll into 6 pieces, sprinkle with scallions, drizzle with the mayonnaise sauce, and serve.

# Sweet-and-sour pork roll

**Yield:** 2 big rolls or 12 pieces

**Prep time:** 25 minutes

**Cook time:** 5 minutes

**Ingredients:**

- 1 tablespoon vegetable oil

- ½ (12-ounce) can spam, diced

- ¼ onion, sliced

- ¼ cup sweet-and-sour sauce, plus more for dressing the roll

- 2 whole nori sheets

- 2 cups sushi rice

- ½ cup chopped pineapple

- 2 scallions, both white and green parts, chopped

**Directions:**

1. In a skillet, heat the vegetable oil over medium heat until it shimmers. Add the spam and the onion, and cook for 3 minutes. Add the sweet-and-sour sauce and stir-fry for 2 minutes, until the spam and onion are well coated, then remove from the heat.

2. Lay out the makisu on a work surface and place one sheet of nori on top, shiny side down. Spread 1 cup of rice evenly over the nori. Put a piece of plastic wrap or parchment paper (about the same size as the makisu) on the rice and flip so the nori side is up.

3. Place half of the cooked meat mixture in a line across the middle of the nori, and lay ¼ cup of the pineapple below the meat.

4. Pick up the edge of the makisu and nori into a tight jelly roll. Let it sit, seam-side down, for about 5 minutes at room temperature.

5. Make another roll with the remaining nori, rice, and filling.

6. Cut each sushi roll into 6 pieces, sprinkle with the scallions, drizzle with the sauce, and serve.

# Ginger chicken roll

**Yield:** 2 big rolls or 12 pieces

**Prep time:** 30 minutes, plus 15 minutes to marinate

**Cook time:** 10 minutes

**Ingredients:**

- 6 ounces boneless, skinless chicken thighs, cut into ½-inch-wide strips
- 2 teaspoons peeled, grated fresh ginger
- 2 tablespoons soy sauce (gluten-free if necessary)
- 2 tablespoons cooking sake
- 1 tablespoon mirin
- 1 tablespoon toasted sesame oil
- 2 whole nori sheets
- 2 cups sushi rice
- 4 tablespoons roasted sesame seeds
- ¼ onion, thinly sliced
- ½ cup shredded red cabbage
- 2 scallions, both white and green parts, chopped mayonnaise

**Directions:**

1. In a large bowl, combine the chicken, ginger, soy sauce, cooking sake, and mirin. Stir until the chicken is coated. Refrigerate to marinate for at least 15 minutes.

2. In a skillet, heat the sesame oil over medium heat until it shimmers. Add the chicken with the marinade and cook for 7 minutes, stirring continuously, until the chicken is cooked through.

3. Lay out the makisu on a work surface and place one sheet of nori on top, shiny side down. Spread 1 cup of rice evenly over the nori. Sprinkle 2 tablespoons of sesame seeds on top. Put a piece of plastic wrap or parchment paper (about the same size as the makisu) on the rice and flip so the nori side is up.

4. Place half of the chicken in a line across the middle of the nori, and lay half of the onion and ¼ cup of the red cabbage below the chicken.

5. Pick up the edge of the makisu and nori into a tight jelly roll. Let it sit, seam-side down, for about 5 minutes at room temperature. Make another roll with the remaining nori, rice, sesame seeds, and filling. Cut each sushi roll into 6 pieces, sprinkle with the scallions, drizzle with the mayonnaise, and serve.

# Sweet-and-sour pork roll

**Yield:** 2 big rolls or 12 pieces

**Prep time:** 25 minutes

**Cook time:** 5 minutes

**Ingredients:**

- 1 tablespoon vegetable oil

- ½ (12-ounce) can spam, diced

- ¼ onion, sliced

- ¼ cup sweet-and-sour sauce, plus more for dressing the roll

- 2 whole nori sheets

- 2 cups sushi rice

- ½ cup chopped pineapple

- 2 scallions, both white and green parts, chopped

**Directions:**

1. In a skillet, heat the vegetable oil over medium heat until it shimmers. Add the spam and the onion, and cook for 3 minutes. Add the sweet-and-sour sauce and stir-fry for 2 minutes, until the spam and onion are well coated, then remove from the heat.

2. Lay out the makisu on a work surface and place one sheet of nori on top, shiny side down. Spread 1 cup of rice evenly over the nori. Put a piece of plastic wrap or parchment paper (about the same size as the makisu) on the rice and flip so the nori side is up.

3. Place half of the cooked meat mixture in a line across the middle of the nori, and lay ¼ cup of the pineapple below the meat.

4. Pick up the edge of the makisu and nori into a tight jelly roll. Let it sit, seam-side down, for about 5 minutes at room temperature.

5. Make another roll with the remaining nori, rice, and filling.

6. Cut each sushi roll into 6 pieces, sprinkle with the scallions, drizzle with the sauce, and serve.

# **Sushi rice**

**Yield:** 4 cups (4 big rolls or 8 thin rolls or 48 pieces nigiri sushi)

**Prep time:** 25 minutes

**Cook time:** 25 minutes

**Ingredients:**

- 1½ cups short-grain white rice
- 1⅔ cups water
- Tablespoons rice vinegar
- 5 teaspoons sugar
- Teaspoons salt
- 1 (4-by-4-inch) piece dried kelp (dashi kombu)

**Directions:**

1. In a fine-mesh strainer set atop a bowl, rinse the rice under cool running water while stirring it with your hand. Drain the rice as soon as the water in the bowl turns a murky white color. Repeat until the water in the bowl is clear.

2. In a medium bowl, combine the rice and water and let soak for 15 minutes at room temperature.

3. In a small bowl, mix the rice vinegar, sugar, and salt. Set aside.

4. Pour the rice and water into a deep saucepan and add the kelp. Cover the pan and bring the mixture to a boil over high heat. Turn the heat to low and cook for 10 minutes. When there is no water left in the pan, turn off the heat, put a kitchen towel under the lid, and steam the rice for 10 minutes.

5. Remove the kelp and discard. Transfer the rice to a large mixing bowl. Add the vinegar mixture to the bowl. Using a rice paddle, fold gently to combine and coat each grain of rice with the mixture

6. (it is like mixing whipped egg whites into cake batter). Cover with a damp, clean cloth and allow to cool to room temperature before using the rice to make sushi.

**Cooking tip:** check the inside of the pan before throwing a kitchen towel over the rice. Put the lid back on if there is already water visible in the pan and cook for 2 more minutes, then check again.

**Storage tip:** move the sushi rice to a bag or glass jar in the fridge. Hold and use in the freezer within 3 weeks. Microwave the rice for 2 to 3 minutes on a microwave-safe dish, sealed, to thaw it. Move the sushi rice to a clean container, cover it, and refrigerate it for preservation in the freezer—usage within a half-day span.

**How to avoid misshapen sushi rolls**

When preparing sushi rolls, typical issue sushi beginners face is that the sushi nori sheet cracks, don't seal, or falls apart. Here are some fantastic answers to these problems:

- Spread the sushi rice appropriately on the nori mat. I propose spreading 1 cup of sushi rice over a whole sheet of nori (or 1/2 cup of sushi rice over a half sheet of nori). Depending upon the recipe, this number can fluctuate a bit. Spreading the rice equally requires a bit of preparation. The roll would not close or be too loose whether there is too much or too little rice. For beginners, however, i strongly suggest that you steadily scatter the rice on the nori sheet until you can't see the nori between the rice grains.

- Pick the right loading quantity and do not overfill. Too much filling induces splitting or opening of sushi rolls. Basically, begin with the filling in a close pile on the rice for a thin roll. The height of the filling pile may be less than a quarter of the thickness of the short side of the sheet of nori.

- Firmly roll. Although when the volume of rice and filling is sufficient, the rolls will not stay together if you roll loosely.

- Create loads of salmon rolls. Training adds to mastering.

**Food safety:** since sushi involves raw fish and vegetables, washing your hands regularly and utilizing multiple cutting boards for each form of ingredient is quite necessary (fish, shellfish, vegetables).

# Preparing seafood

To make a perfect final show, here are useful tips about how to thaw and cut seafood. The exact cutting processes mentioned here are not completely mandatory, but when you obey these instructions, you can have a lot simpler time making sushi.

**Sashimi-grade tuna and salmon**

1. To thaw, place unpackaged frozen fillets on a plate, cover, and refrigerate for about 10 hours.

2. To remove fishy odor, wash the fillets quickly under running water and gently pat dry with paper towels.

3. Cut at a right angle to the grain. For sashimi dishes, slice into approximately 1-by-2-inch pieces that are ⅓ inch thick (1). For nigiri sushi, slice in approximately 1-by-2-inch pieces that are ¼ inch thick (2). For sushi rolls, cut the fish into ½-inch-thick and 2½-inch-long sticks (3). When cutting fish for all types of sushi, carefully pull the knife toward you in one motion, so the fillet doesn't tear.

**Shrimp**

1. If the shrimp are frozen, soak in salt water (1 tablespoon salt  per 2 cups water) and keep in the refrigerator for 1 to 2 hours to thaw.

2. In a bowl, place the thawed shrimp (regardless of whether the shell is on or off) and sprinkle with baking soda (2 tablespoons baking soda per pound). Toss to coat for 1 minute and rinse well with water. Lay the shrimp on paper towels and use more paper towels to blot.

3. Cut the tip of the tail off (if it is tail-on) and scrape off the water on the trail with a knife. This helps remove the fishy smell and avoid oil splatters when it is fried.

4. For nigiri sushi, use shell-on, tail-on, un-deveined medium-size shrimp. For sushi rolls, use deveined medium or large shrimp. If you prefer that the tail stick out from your sushi roll for the final presentation, choose tail-on shrimp.

**Scallops**

1. To thaw, place unpackaged frozen scallops on a plate, cover, and keep in the refrigerator for 4 to 5 hours.

2. Pat the thawed scallops dry with a paper towel. Do not rinse with water because scallops can become bland easily.

3. For sashimi dishes, halve the scallops horizontally. For nigiri sushi, make an incision from the side and butterfly.

**Salmon roe**

Store-bought jarred salmon roe basically does not require preparation. But taste it before serving. If you find the taste is too salty, you can soak the roe in saltwater (1 teaspoon salt per 1 cup water) for about 30 minutes. Drain and gently pat dry with a paper towel.

# Preparing vegetables and other common items

**Avocado**

For sushi rolls, cut into quarters lengthwise, remove the pit, peel, and slice lengthwise. For use as a topping, cut in half lengthwise and remove the pit. Using the knife tip, score the avocado flesh without piercing the skin and scoop it out with a spoon.

**Cucumber**

Use persian cucumber (baby cucumber) that has low moisture, so the sushi roll doesn't become soggy. For sushi rolls, halve lengthwise, then halve lengthwise again to make sticks. To use cucumber to cover a sushi roll as a topping, slice lengthwise with a peeler or slicer. For garnishing sashimi dishes, slice diagonally or use a small cookie cutter to make decorative shapes.

**Imitation crabmeat**

For sushi rolls, halve lengthwise if the imitation crabmeat is leg-style. When the imitation crabmeat is flaked, cut into ½-inch pieces.

**Leaf lettuce**

Wash each leaf and pat dry with a paper towel. For thin sushi rolls, halve lengthwise. For big rolls, if the leaf is shorter than the sushi nori, use without cutting. For garnishing sashimi dishes, tear into palm-sized pieces and lay some sashimi on the lettuce.

**Sushi nori**

Place the shiny nori side down and put sushi rice on the rough side of the nori. For thick (big) sushi rolls, use a whole sheet (about 7 by 8 inches). For thin rolls, halve the sheet on the long side. For gunkanmaki, cut the long side of the sheet into six equal lengths. For hand-rolled sushi, cut the sheet into quarters, so each piece of nori is approximately square.

**Daikon radish**

For garnishing sashimi dishes, shred thinly. Traditionally, daikon should be prepared like a zucchini noodle. The surface of a ½-inch-thick columnar daikon radish should be spirally stripped toward the center (this is called katsuramuki), then the daikon sheet should be cut, so it looks like a noodle. Lay some sashimi on the shredded daikon.

# Sashimi, nigiri, and other sushi dishes

# Sashimi

**Yield:** 4 pieces

**Prep time:** 10 minutes

**Cook time:** 8 minutes

**Ingredients:**

- 1 green leaf lettuce leaf, torn into 4 pieces
- 4 sashimi-grade scallops, halved horizontally
- 1 teaspoon natural sea salt
- 4 tablespoons salmon roe wasabi

**Directions:**

1. Line a serving plate with lettuce, put 2 slices of scallop on each piece of lettuce, and place the salt on the corner of the plate.
2. Place 1 tablespoon of salmon roe on a deep, small plate and put a dash of wasabi on top. Repeat for three more plates with the remaining salmon roe and wasabi.

**Substitution tip:** if you can find japanese shiso (perilla), substitute it for the green leaf lettuce.

# Assorted sashimi

**Yield:** 8 pieces

**Prep time:** 10 minutes

**Cook time:** 5 minutes

**Ingredients:**

- Green leaf lettuce leaf, torn
- ¼ small daikon radish, shredded
- ½ pound sashimi-grade tuna, sliced
- 2 teaspoon wasabis
- ½ pound seared bonito, sliced into ⅓ -inch-wide pieces
- Soy sauce (gluten-free if necessary)
- ½ pound sashimi-grade salmon, sliced

**Directions:**

1. Line a serving plate with the daikon, arrange the lettuce on the daikon, and make the wasabi into a mound on the corner.
2. Place the sliced tuna, salmon, and bonito on the lettuce.
3. Serve with a small, shallow dish of soy sauce for each person.

**Substitution tip:** if you can find japanese shiso (perilla), substitute it for green leaf lettuce.

# Nigiri sushi

**Yield:** 10 to 12 pieces

**Prep time:** 20 minutes

**Cook time:**   10 minutes

**Ingredients:**

- 2 cups sushi rice
- Wasabi
- ½ pound sashimi-grade tuna, sliced
- 2 tablespoons pickled sushi ginger
- Soy sauce (gluten-free if necessary)

**Directions:**

1. Scoop 1 heaping tablespoon of sushi rice on your wet hand and make it into a flat football shape.
2. Place a dash of wasabi on the center of the rice, cover with a slice of tuna, gently press the fish down on the rice, and transfer it to a serving plate. Repeat with the remaining rice, wasabi, and tuna.
3. Put the ginger on the corner of the plate (or in a small bowl alongside) and serve with a small, shallow dish of soy sauce for each person.

**Cooking tip:** wet your hands and the tablespoon before touching the sushi rice, so the rice doesn't stick.

**Ingredient tip:** if you prefer not to use wasabi, skip that part of the step.

# Japanese egg omelet nigiri

**Yield:** 10 pieces

**Prep time:** 20 minutes

**Cook time:** 12 minutes

**Ingredients:**

- Japanese egg omelet cut crosswise into ten ½-inch-wide pieces
- 2 cups sushi rice
- Soy sauce (gluten-free if necessary)
- 10 (½-by-4-inch) nori strips

**Directions:**

1. Divide the rice into 10 portions, place each into wet hands, and make it into a flat football shape.
2. Place a piece of omelet on each piece of shaped rice.
3. Fasten the omelet in place using one nori strip crossways with the seam on the bottom. Place the sushi seam-side down on a serving plate. Repeat with the remaining rice, omelet pieces, and nori strips.
4. Serve with a small, shallow dish of soy sauce for each person.

# Salmon nigiri with marinated sweet onion

**Yield:** 10 to 12 pieces

**Prep time:** 20 minutes

**Cook time:** 8 minutes

**Ingredients:**

- ½ pound sashimi-grade salmon, sliced
- Soy sauce (gluten-free if necessary)
- 2 cups sushi rice
- ¼ cup marinated sweet onion

**Directions:**

1. Scoop 1 heaping tablespoon of sushi rice on your wet hand and make it into a flat football shape.
2. Place a slice of salmon on the rice and top with 1 teaspoon of onion. Repeat with the remaining rice, salmon, and onion.
3. Serve with a small, shallow dish of soy sauce for each person.

# Boiled shrimp nigiri

**Yield:** 10 pieces

**Prep time:** 35 minutes

**Cook time:** 5 minutes

**Ingredients:**

- 2 cups sushi rice

- Soy sauce (gluten-free if necessary)

- Wasabi

- 10 medium shell-on, tail-on shrimp, prepared

**Directions:**

1. Fill a deep pan with water and bring it to a boil over high heat.

2. Meanwhile, slowly insert a skewer in the shrimp from head to tail beneath the shell on the belly (leg) side to prevent it from curling when cooked. Boil five skewered shrimp at a time over medium heat for 2 to 3 minutes, or until they turn pink.

3. Once it cools enough to handle, remove the shell and legs, and make an incision from the belly side and butterfly. After it is opened, if you see back veins, gently remove them.

4. Divide the rice into 10 portions. With wet hands, form each portion into a flat football shape.

5. Place a dash of wasabi on the center of the rice and cover it with a piece of shrimp. Repeat with the remaining rice, wasabi, and shrimp.

6. Serve with a small, shallow dish of soy sauce for each person.

**Cooking tip:** you can devein shrimp using a toothpick without cutting, but this requires a little technique. For nigiri shrimp, it is easiest to devein after butterflying.

# Scallop nigiri

**Yield:** 10 pieces

**Prep time:** 20 minutes

**Ingredients:**

- 2 tablespoons pickled sushi ginger

- Wasabi

- 2 cups sushi rice

- 10 scallops, butterflied

- Natural sea salt

**Directions:**

1. Divide the rice into 10 portions, place each into wet hands, and make it into a flat football shape.

2. Place a dash of wasabi on the center of the rice, cover with a scallop, and transfer to a serving plate. Repeat with the remaining rice, wasabi, and scallops.

3. Put the ginger on the corner of the plate and serve with a small, shallow dish of salt for each person.

# Chicken teriyaki nigiri

**Yield:** 10 to 12 pieces

**Prep time:** 25 minutes

**Cook time:** 15 minutes

**Ingredients:**

- 1 tablespoon vegetable oil
- 2 medium boneless, skinless chicken thighs
- ½ tablespoon cooking sake, plus 1 teaspoon
- ½ tablespoon soy sauce (gluten-free if necessary)
- ½ tablespoon mirin
- ½ teaspoon sugar
- 2 cups sushi rice
- 10 (½-by-4-inch) nori strips

**Directions:**

1. In a skillet, heat the vegetable oil over medium heat until it shimmers. Add the chicken and cook for 4 minutes. Flip the chicken, add ½ tablespoon of cooking sake, cover the skillet, and reduce the heat to low. Steam the chicken for 3 minutes.

2. Add the remaining 1 teaspoon of cooking sake, the soy sauce, mirin, and sugar. Increase the heat to medium and simmer for 6 minutes, turning the chicken occasionally and using a spoon to baste it with the sauce frequently, until the sauce is almost  completely reduced. Let it cool and slice into ½-inch-thick pieces.

3. Scoop 1 heaping tablespoon of sushi rice onto your wet hand and make it into a flat football shape. Place a piece of chicken on the rice. Fasten the chicken in place using 1 nori strip crossways with the seam on the bottom. Place the sushi seam-side down on a serving plate. Repeat with the remaining rice, chicken, and nori.

# Beef with scallion nigiri

**Yield:** 10 to 12 pieces

**Prep time:** 20 minutes

**Cook time:** 10 minutes

**Ingredients:**

- 2 scallions, both white and green parts, chopped
- ¼ teaspoon wasabi
- 6 ounces sirloin steak, chuck steak, or rib-eye steak, sliced into 1-by-2-inch pieces, ¼ to ½ inch thick
- 2 tablespoon soy sauce (gluten-free if necessary)
- 2 cups sushi rice

**Directions:**

1. Heat a dry skillet over medium heat for a few minutes, then cook the beef on one side for 3 to 4 minutes.
2. Meanwhile, mix the wasabi and soy sauce.
3. Flip the beef, add the sauce, and cook for another 3 to 4 minutes until it turns brown. Set aside.
4. Scoop 1 heaping tablespoon of sushi rice on your wet hand and make it into a flat football shape. Repeat with the remaining rice.
5. Once the beef cools enough to handle, place a piece on each mound of shaped rice, transfer to a serving dish, and sprinkle with the scallions.

**Cooking tip:** if the skillet is too small to cook all the beef at once, cook it in batches.

**Ingredient tip:** if you use leaner meat, heat ½ tablespoon oil in the skillet until it shimmers before adding the beef to the pan.

# Spam nigiri

**Yield:** 10 pieces

**Prep time:** 25 minutes

**Cook time:** 5 minutes

**Ingredients:**

- 10 (½-by-4-inch) nori strips
- 2 cups sushi rice
- 1 (12-ounce) can spam, sliced into 10 pieces

**Directions:**

1. Heat a dry skillet over medium heat for a few minutes, then cook the spam for 3 to 4 minutes, flipping halfway through the cooking time, until it is browned.

2. Divide the rice into 10 portions. Place each portion into wet hands, and make it into a flat football shape.

3. Fasten the spam in place using 1 nori strip crossways with the seam on the bottom. Place the sushi seam-side down on a serving plate. Repeat with the remaining rice, spam, and nori.

# Temari sushi

# Marinated tuna (zuke-maguro) temari

**Yield:** 12 pieces

**Prep time:** 55 minutes

**Cook time:** 5 minutes

**Ingredients:**

- 8 ounces sashimi-grade tuna, sliced thinly
- 2 scallions, both white and green parts, chopped
- 2 cups sushi rice
- Roasted white sesame seeds
- 2 tablespoons cooking sake
- 2 tablespoons mirin
- 4 tablespoons soy sauce (gluten-free if necessary)

**Directions:**

1. In a small saucepan, stir together the soy sauce, cooking sake, and mirin. Bring the mixture to a boil over medium-high heat. Turn the heat to low and cook for 3 minutes. Turn off the heat, allow the pan to cool for 1 or 2 minutes, and transfer to the refrigerator and let it cool for about 15 minutes.

2. After cooling, remove the pan from the refrigerator, add the tuna, and flip until it is coated completely with the sauce. Marinate for 20 minutes in the refrigerator.

3. On a piece of plastic wrap (about 6 by 6 inches), place 1 slice of marinated tuna; put 1 heaping tablespoon of the rice on the tuna.

4. Hold up the four corners of the wrap with one hand and twist the sushi tightly with the other hand to make a ball shape. Transfer the sushi to a serving plate. Repeat with the remaining tuna slices and rice. Sprinkle with the sesame seeds and scallions.

# Smoked salmon temari with cucumber

**Yield:** 12 pieces

**Prep time:** 25 minutes

**Cook time:** 15 minutes

**Ingredients:**

- 2 cups sushi rice

- Baby cucumber thinly sliced lengthwise

- 12 slices smoked salmon slices, each 2 to 3 inches long

**Directions:**

1. On a 6-by-6-inch piece of plastic wrap or damp cheesecloth, place 1 slice of smoked salmon. Scoop 1 heaping tablespoon of rice on the salmon.

2. Hold up the four corners of the wrapper with one hand and twist the sushi tightly with the other hand to make a ball shape. Transfer the sushi to a serving plate. Repeat with the remaining salmon slices and rice.

3. Top each piece of sushi with one slice of cucumber. The sushi can be eaten on its own.

**Ingredient tip:** if you use cheesecloth to shape the sushi, you can keep rice from sticking to it by wringing out the cloth with water after every 2 or 3 pieces you make.

**Serving tip:** smoked salmon has a delicious taste and flavor, so the sushi can be eaten on its own. Serve with a small, shallow dish of soy sauce, if necessary.

# Egg and salmon roe temari

**Yield:** 10 pieces

**Prep time:** 25 minutes

**Cook time:** 10 minutes

**Ingredients:**

- Nonstick cooking spray
- 1 teaspoon water
- 2 eggs, beaten
- 3 tablespoons salmon roe
- 3 cups sushi rice
- 1 teaspoon cornstarch

**Directions:**

1. In a small bowl, whisk together the cornstarch and water. Mix the cornstarch mixture into the beaten eggs.

2. Heat a 10-inch skillet over medium-high heat and coat with cooking spray. Pour half of the egg mixture into the skillet and spread the egg all over the surface of the pan to make a thin layer. Cook over low heat for about 3 minutes, gently flipping halfway through the cooking time with a rubber spatula. Make another thin fried egg with the remaining egg mixture.

3. Transfer the fried eggs to a cutting board, cut each lengthwise into three equal pieces, then cut each piece crosswise into three pieces to create 18 approximately equal-sized pieces.

4. On a 6-by-6-inch piece of plastic wrap or damp cheesecloth, place 1 piece of egg and scoop 1 heaping tablespoon of the rice on the egg.

5. Hold up the four corners of the wrapper with one hand and twist the sushi tightly with the other hand to make a ball shape. Transfer the sushi to a serving plate. Repeat with the remaining egg pieces and rice.

6. Top each sushi with ½ teaspoon of salmon roe.

**Cooking tip:** the cornstarch keeps the thin fried egg from tearing. However, when it is cooked too long, the egg crisps and can shatter.

# Temaki sushi

# Traditional hand-rolled sushi

**Yield:** 8 rolls

**Prep time:** 40 minutes

**Cook time:** 20 minutes

**Ingredients:**

- Parsley

- 2 cups sushi rice

- ¼ pound sashimi-grade salmon, sliced

- 2 whole nori sheets

- ¼ pound sashimi-grade tuna, sliced

- Soy sauce (gluten-free if necessary)

**Directions:**

1. Put a piece of nori on your palm and spread 2 tablespoons of rice on it with a wet spoon.

2. Dip a piece of tuna and salmon in soy sauce, and arrange each piece with 1 sprig of parsley diagonally across the middle of the rice. Roll into a cone shape. Repeat with the remaining nori, rice, and tuna and salmon slices.

# Beef with lettuce temaki

**Yield:** 8 rolls

**Prep time:** 40 minutes

**Cook time:** 10 minutes

**Ingredients:**

- 4 ounces sirloin steak, chuck steak, or rib-eye steak, cut into ½-inch-thick and 2½-inchlong stick
- Salt
- Freshly ground black pepper
- 2 whole nori sheets,
- 2 cups sushi rice
- 2 green leaf lettuce leaves, torn into palm-size pieces ¼ cup marinated sweet onion

**Directions:**

1. Heat a dry skillet over medium heat for a few minutes, and cook the beef for about 7 minutes or until it turns brown. Season with the salt and pepper halfway through the cooking time. Set aside.

2. Put a piece of nori in your palm, spread 2 tablespoons of the rice over it with a wet spoon, and place the lettuce on the rice.

3. Arrange a stack of beef and about ½ tablespoon of onion diagonally across the middle of the lettuce. Roll into a cone  shape.

4. Repeat with the remaining nori, rice, and filling.

# Salad temaki

**Yield:** 8 rolls

**Prep time:** 40 minutes

**Cook time:** 15 minutes

**Ingredients:**

- 2 cups sushi rice

- Japanese egg omelet

- 8 teaspoons mayonnaise

- 2 whole nori sheets, cut

- 1 baby cucumber, cut into thin strips

- 8 pieces leg-style imitation crabmeat

**Directions:**

1. Cut the omelet into quarters lengthwise and halve each quarter  crosswise. Set aside.

2. Put a piece of nori in your palm and spread 2 tablespoons of the rice over it with a wet spoon.

3. Arrange 1 piece of omelet, 1 piece of imitation crabmeat, and some sliced cucumber diagonally across the middle of the rice. Put 1 teaspoon of mayonnaise on the cucumber. Roll into a cone shape.

4. Repeat with the remaining nori, rice, and filling.

# Staples and sauces

# Spicy mayonnaise sauce

**Yield** : about ⅓ cup

**Prep time:** 5 minutes

**Cook time:** 3 minutes

**Ingredients:**

- ¼ cup mayonnaise

- 1 tablespoon sriracha sauce

- 1 teaspoon toasted sesame oil

**Directions:**

1.  In a small bowl, mix the mayonnaise, sriracha sauce, and sesame oil.

# Ginger dressing

**Yield:** 1½ cup

**Prep time:** 10 minutes

**Cook time:** 5 minutes

**Ingredients:**

- 1 large carrot, coarsely chopped
- ½ large onion, coarsely chopped
- 1 (3- to 4-inch) piece fresh ginger, peeled and coarsely chopped
- 1 garlic clove
- ¼ cup soy sauce (gluten-free if necessary)
- ¼ cup of rice vinegar
- ½ teaspoon salt
- 1 tablespoon toasted sesame oil ½ cup extra-virgin olive oil

**Directions:**

1. In a food processor, combine the carrot, onion, ginger, garlic, soy sauce, rice vinegar, salt, sesame oil, and olive oil. Blend until somewhat smooth.
2. Transfer to a jar, cover, and keep refrigerated. Use within 2 weeks.

**Cooking tip:** on the first day, the vegetables and the oil may seem barely mixed, but the dressing reaches the right consistency after a few days.

# Japanese egg omelet

**Yield:** 1 omelet or 10 pieces for nigiri or 4 sticks for sushi rolls

**Prep time:** 5 minutes

**Cook time:** 5 minutes

**Ingredients:**

- 3 large eggs, beaten
- 2 teaspoons soy sauce (gluten-free if necessary)
- Nonstick cooking spray

**Directions:**

**To make the traditional version**

1. In a mixing bowl, stir together the eggs and soy sauce.
2. Coat a preheated nonstick rectangular skillet (5 to 6 inches by 7 inches) with cooking spray and pour one-third of the egg mixture into the skillet, being sure to spread the egg over the entire surface of the pan. Cook over medium heat for 20 seconds until the edge of the egg is cooked and liquid is still present on top.
3. Fold the egg in three. It is okay if the egg is unshaped at this moment. Slide the egg to the far side of the pan.
4. Pour half of the remaining mixture into the empty space of the pan, lift the existing egg omelet, and let the mixture flow  underneath while spreading the egg all over the surface of the pan. Cook for 30 seconds and fold into three again, then slide the egg to the far side of the pan. Repeat with the remaining egg mixture. Gently press the omelet with the spatula, and cook for 30 seconds on each side.

**To make an easier version**

1. In a mixing bowl, stir together the eggs and soy sauce.
2. Coat a preheated 8-inch nonstick skillet with cooking spray and pour all of the egg mixtures into the skillet. Cook over medium-low heat for 1 minute, without stirring, and until the edges of the eggs are slightly cooked.
3. Using a spatula, gently gather the cooked part toward the center of the skillet and spread the uncooked egg toward the edges of the pan. Cook for 1 minute until the egg is set.

4.  Fold the egg in three, gently press the omelet with the spatula, and cook for 30 seconds on each side.

5.  Place the makisu on a work surface and cover with a piece of parchment paper or paper towel. Lay the omelet on it and wrap it with the makisu to make a 1-inch-thick rectangle. Let it sit for 10 minutes at room temperature.

**Cooking tip:** the omelet, wrapped in the makisu, can be stored in the refrigerator for about 2 hours to cool, so the omelet acquires a firmer shape.

# Tempura batter

**Yield:** 1 cup

**Prep time:** 10 minutes

**Cook time:** 5 minutes

**Ingredients:**

- ½ cup cornstarch
- 1 teaspoon rice vinegar
- 1 teaspoon salt
- ½ cup of cold water

**Directions:**

1. In a small bowl, stir together the cornstarch, rice vinegar, salt, and cold water, and stir very gently until just a few lumps are left.

# Ponzu sauce

**Yield** : ½ cup

**Prep time:** 5 minutes

**Cook time:** 3 minutes

**Ingredients:**

- ¼ cup soy sauce (gluten-free if necessary)
- ¼ cup of rice vinegar
- Juice of ½ lime

**Directions:**

1. Combine the soy sauce, rice vinegar, and lime juice in a jar and keep in the refrigerator for up to 2 weeks.

# Sweet eel sauce

**Gluten-free, nut-free, vegan**

This sauce has a perfect sweet-savory taste and a thick texture. Because the sauce needs to be cooked to get the right consistency, you might want to make this sauce first in your cooking process. Or you can make this sauce ahead of time, keep it in the refrigerator, and use it within 1 month. If the sauce becomes very thick in the refrigerator, keep it at room temperature for at least 1 hour before you use it.

**Yield:** ½ cup

**Prep time:** 10 minutes

**Cook time:** 25 minutes

**Ingredients:**

- ½ cup soy sauce (gluten-free if necessary)
- ½ cup mirin
- ¼ cup cooking sake
- 2 tablespoons sugar

**Directions:**

1. In a saucepan, stir together the soy sauce, mirin, cooking sake, and sugar. Bring it to a boil over medium heat. Reduce the heat to low, simmer for 20 minutes, and occasionally stir until thickened. Let it cool for 10 minutes at room temperature.

2. Place the mixture in a sterilized 4-ounce dressing bottle and store it in the refrigerator for up to 1 month.

# Spicy mango sauce

**Yield:** 1 cup

**Prep time:** 10 minutes

**Cook time:** 5 minutes

**Ingredients:**

- 1 large mango, peeled and diced
- 5 cilantro sprigs, trimmed and finely minced
- ½ teaspoon salt
- Pinch freshly ground black pepper
- 2 teaspoons crushed red pepper
- 2 teaspoons rice vinegar
- Teaspoon grated garlic
- Teaspoons honey
- 2 teaspoons freshly squeezed lemon juice

**Directions:**

1. in a mixing bowl, stir together the mango, cilantro, salt, black pepper, red pepper, vinegar, garlic, honey, and lemon juice.
2. transfer to an 8-ounce jar, cover, and keep in the refrigerator for up to 1 week.

# Pico de gallo

**Yield:** 2 cups

**Prep time:** 10 minutes

**Cook time:** 5 minutes

**Ingredients:**

- 2 large tomatoes, seeded and diced
- 10 cilantro sprigs, trimmed and minced
- ½ red onion, diced
- 2 teaspoons grated garlic
- ½ teaspoon salt
- ½ jalapeño, seeded and finely diced
- Juice of 1 lime

**Directions:**

1. In a mixing bowl, stir together the tomatoes, cilantro, onion, garlic, salt, jalapeño, and lime juice.

2. Transfer to a 16-ounce jar, cover, and keep in the refrigerator for up to 1 week.

# Tempura dashi sauce

**Yield:** 1 cup

**Prep time:** 5 minutes

**Cook time:** 5 minutes

**Ingredients:**

- 1 cup of water
- 1 teaspoon shimaya kombu dashi soup stock powder, or any vegetable - or fish -based dashi powder
- ¼ cup soy sauce (gluten-free if necessary)
- ¼ cup mirin

**Directions:**

1. In a saucepan, stir together the water, dashi powder, soy sauce, and mirin. Bring to a boil over medium heat. Let it cool down.
2. Transfer to an 8-ounce jar, cover, and keep in the refrigerator for up to 1 month.

# Sweet-and-sour sauce

**Yield** : ¼ cup

**Prep time:** 5 minutes

**Cook time:** 5 minutes

**Ingredients:**

- 2 tablespoons sweet chili sauce
- 1 tablespoon ketchup
- 1 tablespoon soy sauce (gluten-free if necessary)

**Directions:**

1. Combine the chili sauce, ketchup, and soy sauce.
2. Transfer to a 4-ounce jar and keep in the refrigerator for up to 2 weeks.

# Miso sesame sauce

**Yield:** 1/3 cup

**Prep time:** 5 minutes

**Cook time:** 5 minutes

**Ingredients:**

- 2 tablespoons roasted sesame seeds
- 2 tablespoons miso paste
- 2 teaspoons toasted sesame oil
- 1 tablespoon sugar
- 2 teaspoons water

**Directions:**

1. In a mixing bowl, stir together the sesame seeds, miso, sesame oil, and sugar. Whisk in the water until you have a consistency you like.

2. Transfer to a 4-ounce jar and keep in the refrigerator for up to 3 weeks.

# Peanut sauce

**Yield:** 1/3 cups

**Prep time:** 5 minutes

**Cook time:** 5 minutes

**Ingredients:**

- 2 tablespoons no-sugar-added and no-salt-added peanut butter
- 1 tablespoon soy sauce (gluten-free if necessary)
- 1 teaspoon cumin
- 1 teaspoon peeled, grated fresh ginger
- 1 teaspoon grated garlic
- 1 teaspoon toasted sesame oil
- 1 teaspoon onion powder
- Juice of ½ lemon
- Salt
- Freshly ground black pepper
- 3 tablespoons warm water, as needed

**Directions:**

1. In a mixing bowl, stir together the peanut butter, soy sauce, cumin, ginger, garlic, sesame oil, onion powder, and lemon juice. Taste and season with salt and black pepper as needed. Whisk in the warm water until you have a consistency you like.

2. Transfer to a 4-ounce container and keep in the refrigerator for up to 2 weeks.

# Pickling liquid

**Yield:** 1 cup

**Prep time:** 5 minutes

**Cook time:** 3 minutes

**Ingredients:**

- ½ cup toasted sesame oil
- ¼ cup soy sauce (gluten-free if necessary)
- ¼ cup of rice vinegar
- ½ teaspoon salt
- 1 teaspoon peeled, grated fresh ginger

**Directions:**

1. Combine the sesame oil, soy sauce, rice vinegar, salt, and ginger in an 8-ounce jar. Cover and shake to combine.
2. Store in the refrigerator for up to 3 weeks.

# Almond sauce

**Yield:** ¼ cup

**Prep time:** 5 minutes

**Cook time:** 3 minutes

**Ingredients:**

- 2 tablespoon no-sugar-added and no-salt-added almond butter
- Juice of ½ lemon
- ¼ teaspoon salt
- ½ tablespoon freshly ground black pepper
- ¼ teaspoon onion powder
- ½ teaspoon grated garlic
- 3 tablespoons warm water, as needed

**Directions:**

1. In a mixing bowl, stir together the almond butter, lemon juice, salt, pepper, onion powder, and garlic. Whisk in the warm water until you have a consistency you like.
2. Transfer to a 4-ounce jar and keep in the refrigerator for up to 2 weeks.

# Pickled sushi ginger (gari)

**Yield:** 1/3 cup

**Prep time:** 10 minutes, plus 12 hours to marinate

**Cook time:** 2 minutes

**Ingredients:**

- 3 ounces young ginger
- ½ cup of rice vinegar
- 1 tablespoon sugar
- 1 teaspoon salt

**Directions:**

1. Peel the ginger with a small spoon if it has thick skin. Slice very thinly with a slicer or peeler.

2. Fill a saucepan with water. Bring the water to a boil over high heat, add the ginger, and cook for 2 minutes. Drain and let it cool.

3. Combine the vinegar, sugar, and salt and microwave for 20 seconds to melt the sugar. Mix well.

4. Wring out the ginger by hand and add the ginger and the sauce to a 4-ounce jar. Marinate in the refrigerator for at least 12  hours.

# Tempura batter bits (agedama or tenkasu)

**Yield:** ¼ cup

**Prep time:** 5 minutes

**Cook time:** 15 minutes

**Ingredients:**

- 2 tablespoons cornstarch
- 2 tablespoons water
- ½ teaspoon salt
- Vegetable oil, for frying

**Directions:**

1. In a small bowl, stir together the cornstarch, water, and salt.

2. In a nonstick skillet, heat ½ inch of vegetable oil over medium-low heat until it shimmers. Using a small spoon, put small drops of the mixture in the oil until the dots of the mixture almost cover the bottom of the pan. Fry for 4 to 5 minutes, occasionally stirring, until it browns slightly. Using a mesh skimmer, transfer the bits to a plate lined with paper towels to drain. Repeat with the remaining mixture.

3. When it cools down, transfer to a freezer bag and store in the freezer for up to 1 month. Use without thawing.

# Gunkanmaki sushi

# Buttery corn gunkanmaki

**Yield:** 10 to 12 pieces

**Prep time:** 30 minutes

**Cook time:** 10 minutes

**Ingredients:**

- 2 tablespoons butter or margarine
- 1 cup frozen sweet corn kernels
- 2 tablespoons soy sauce (gluten-free if necessary)
- 2 cups sushi rice
- 2 whole nori sheets

**Directions:**

1. In a skillet, melt the butter over medium-high heat. Add the corn and stir-fry for about 5 minutes to evaporate the water from the frozen corn. Add the soy sauce and stir for 1 minute.

2. Scoop 1 heaping tablespoon of sushi rice on your wet hand and form it into a flat football shape.

3. Wrap a strip of nori around the sides of the rice, shiny-side out, creating a tiny collar all around the rice. It is okay that the  edge of the nori strip doesn't stick firmly.

4. Put 1 tablespoon of the corn on top. Repeat with the remaining rice, nori, and corn.

# Minced tuna and scallion (negitoro) gunkanmaki

**Yield:** 12 pieces

**Prep time:** 40 minutes

**Cook time:** 15 minutes

**Ingredients:**

- ½ pound sashimi-grade tuna
- 1 tablespoon soy sauce (gluten-free if necessary)
- 2 cups sushi rice
- 2 whole nori sheets, cut
- 1 scallion, both white and green parts, chopped

**Directions:**

1. Cut the tuna into small pieces and mince finely. Place in a bowl, mix in the soy sauce and divide into 12 equal portions.
2. Divide the rice into 12 portions, place each portion into your wet hand, and make it into a flat football shape.
3. Wrap a strip of nori around the sides of the rice, shiny-side out, creating a tiny collar all around the rice. It is okay that the edge of the nori strip doesn't stick firmly.
4. Put one portion of the tuna mixture on the rice and top with some chopped scallion. Repeat with the remaining rice, nori, tuna, and scallions.

# Salmon roe (ikura) gunkanmaki

**Yield** : 10 to 12 pieces

**Prep time:** 30 minutes

**Cook time:** 15 minutes

**Ingredients:**

- 2 whole nori sheets, cut.

- 2 cups sushi rice

- 7 ounces salmon roe

**Directions:**

1. Scoop 1 heaping tablespoon of sushi rice on your wet hand and form it into a flat football shape.

2. Wrap a strip of nori around the sides of the rice, shiny-side out, creating a tiny collar all around the rice. It is okay that the edge of the nori strip doesn't stick firmly.

3. Place 1 tablespoon of salmon roe on top of the rice. Repeat with the remaining rice, nori, and salmon roe.

# Lemony crabmeat gunkanmaki

**Yield:** 10 to 12 pieces

**Prep time:** 40 minutes

**Cook time:** 20 minutes

**Ingredients:**

- 1 baby cucumber, sliced diagonally
- 2 salt
- Juice of ½ lemon
- 1 (4¼-ounce) can lump crabmeat, drained
- Freshly ground black pepper
- 2 cups sushi rice
- 2 whole nori sheets, cut

**Directions:**

1. In a bowl, whisk together the crabmeat, a pinch of salt and pepper, and lemon juice. Taste and add more salt and pepper as needed.
2. Scoop 1 heaping tablespoon of sushi rice on your wet hand and form into a flat football shape.
3. Wrap a strip of nori around the sides of the rice, shiny-side out, creating a tiny collar all around the rice. It is okay that the edge of the nori strip doesn't stick firmly.
4. Set 1 or 2 pieces of sliced cucumber on the edge of the rice, and put 2 teaspoons of the crabmeat on the rice. Repeat with the remaining rice, nori, cucumber, and crabmeat.

# Corn and tuna with mayo gunkanmaki

**Yield:** 10 to 12 pieces

**Prep time:** 30 minutes

**Cook time:** 10 minutes

**Ingredients:**

- ½ cup frozen sweet corn kernels
- 1 (5-ounce) can tuna packed in water, drained
- 2 tablespoons mayonnaise
- Salt
- Freshly ground black pepper
- 2 cups sushi rice
- 2 whole nori sheets

**Directions**

1. In a small microwave-safe bowl, microwave the frozen corn, covered, for about 50 seconds.
2. In a small bowl, mix the corn, tuna, and mayonnaise. Taste and season with salt and pepper as needed.
3. Scoop 1 heaping tablespoon of sushi rice on your wet hand and form it into a flat football shape.
4. Wrap a strip of nori around the sides of the rice, shiny-side out, creating a tiny collar all around the rice. It is okay that the edge of the nori strip doesn't stick firmly. Put 1 tablespoon of the tuna mixture on top. Repeat with the remaining rice, nori, and tuna mixture.